DATE DUE

FEB 20 '04			

ASTEROIDS, COMETS, AND METEORS

Carole Marsh

Series Editor:
Arthur Upgren, Professor of Astronomy
Wesleyan University

Twenty-First Century Books

Brookfield, Connecticut

Twenty-First Century Books
A Division of The Millbrook Press
2 Old New Milford Road
Brookfield, CT 06804

Printed in the United States of America

Created and produced in association with Blackbirch Graphics, Inc.

Photo Credits
Cover (background) and page 4: ©NASA; cover (inset) and page 11: ©Ronald E.
Royer/Science Photo Library/Photo Researchers, Inc.; page 6: Royal Observatory,
Edinburgh/AAO/Science Photo Library/Photo Researchers, Inc.; pages 9, 18, 27: North
Wind Picture Archives; pages 12, 50, 53: ©Julian Baum/Science Photo Library/Photo
Researchers, Inc.; page 20: ©Dr. F. Espenak/Science Photo Library/Photo Researchers,
Inc.; page 23: Science Photo Library; page 24: ©NASA/Science Source/Photo
Researchers, Inc.; page 26: AP/Wide World Photos, Inc.; page 30: ©Dr. Seth Shos-
tak/Science Photo Library/Photo Researchers, Inc.; page 32: ©Pekka Parviainen/Science
Photo Library/Photo Researchers, Inc.; page 39: ©Dennis Milon/Science Photo
Library/Photo Researchers, Inc.; page 41: ©H. R. Bramaz/Peter Arnold, Inc.; pages 45, 58:
©NASA/Peter Arnold, Inc.; page 46: ©NASA/Science Photo Library/Photo Researchers,
Inc.; page 54: U.S. Navy/Science Photo Library/Photo Researchers, Inc.

Library of Congress Cataloging-in-Publication Data

Marsh, Carole.
    Asteroids, comets, and meteors / Carole Marsh. — 1st ed.
        p.   cm. — (Secrets of space)
    Includes bibliographical references and index.
    Summary: Describes the properties and observations of comets, meteors, and asteroids and
explores how scientists use these phenomena to learn more about the universe.
    ISBN 0-8050-4473-6
    1. Comets—Juvenile literature. 2. Meteors—Juvenile literature. 3. Asteroids—Juvenile
literature. [1. Comets. 2. Meteors. 3. Asteroids.]   I. Title. II. Series.
QB721.5.M37   1996
523.4'4—dc20   96-8882
                                                                              CIP
                                                                              AC

TABLE OF CONTENTS

INTRODUCTION

Humans have always been fascinated by space, but it has been only since the 1950s that technology has allowed us to actually travel beyond our Earth's atmosphere to explore the universe. What riches of knowledge this space exploration has brought us! All of the planets except Pluto have been mapped extensively, if not completely. Among the planets, only Pluto has not been visited by a space probe, and that will likely change soon. Men have walked on the Moon, and many of the satellites of Jupiter, Saturn, Uranus, and even Neptune have been investigated in detail.

We have learned the precise composition of the Sun and the atmospheres of the planets. We know more about comets, meteors, and asteroids than ever before. And many scientists now think there may be other forms of life in our galaxy and beyond.

In the *Secrets of Space* series, we journey through the wondrous world of space: our solar system, our galaxy, and our universe. It is a world seemingly without end, a world of endless fascination.

—Arthur Upgren
Professor of Astronomy
Wesleyan University

As this 1986 false-color image of Halley's Comet shows, a bright comet streaking through the night sky is an impressive sight.

CHAPTER 1

"TWINKLE, TWINKLE, LITTLE COMET"

Quick! Look up in the sky. It's a comet! Or is it a meteor? Or a meteroid? Perhaps it's an asteroid.

Figuring out what is overhead in the night sky can be confusing. Throughout time, people of all ages have scanned the sky and puzzled over the many mysterious objects they've seen there. Today, scientists can offer surprising answers to age-old questions about comets, meteors, and asteroids.

The search for comets—objects made of ice and dust that orbit the Sun—is undertaken not only by professional scientists but also by eager amateurs. In fact, many amateur comet-hunters have been the first to discover new comets. For example, in 1965, a Japanese boy built a telescope so that he could discover a comet—and he did!

Nothing captures the imagination of sky-gazers more than comets. Early peoples had no idea what comets were or where they came from. Many tried to find ways to explain these streaks of light high above in the sky.

Everyone was curious about these bright passersby in the sky, but even astronomers—scientists who study the universe—did not know what to make of them. Born around the year 460 B.C., the Greek philosopher Democritus thought that a comet was created when "stars" passed near one another. Between the years 1400 B.C. and A.D. 100, Chinese astronomers recorded the appearance of at least 338 comets. And as recently as 1950, American and Russian scientists argued over whether or not comets had originated from the planet Jupiter.

Today, scientists believe that the study of comets will help them learn how the universe began and what its future may be. This is because comets are truly messengers from the past. As they travel, they accumulate interstellar dust. These fine particles of matter may have been created when the universe was born—an estimated 4.6 billion years ago. Comets eventually bring this ancient dust to our solar system. There's no telling what scientists might be able to learn from this dust.

The word *comet* comes from the Greek word *kometes*, which means "hairy." Some early peoples described comets as hairy stars because of the flowing tresses of light that they spew across the sky. The Tshi people of Zaire called comets hair stars. The ancient Chinese labeled comets broom stars, perhaps because the tail looks as if it could sweep the sky clean.

Hundreds of years ago, European monks believed that they could smell a comet coming. Today, scientists refer to comets by the spooky-sounding term *apparition* (which is also used to describe ghosts).

A comet is a celestial body much smaller in size than any planet. In 1950, astronomer Fred Lawrence Whipple figured out that comets had a nucleus made up of what was basically dirty ice. He theorized that, as a comet approached the Sun on its orbit, some of the comet's matter would vaporize. This so-called outgassing could create a rocketlike accelera-

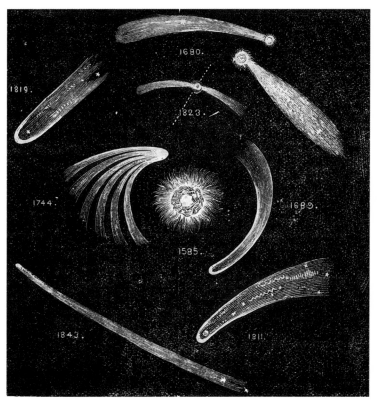

Both astronomers and amateurs have long been fascinated by comets. They have recorded and drawn these celestial bodies for centuries.

tion by the comet, either toward or away from the Sun. This helped to explain the nongravitational forces that affected the movement of comets, which could speed up or delay a comet's orbit around the Sun. These new ideas became known as the icy-conglomerate model.

A comet is made up of three parts: a small center core, or nucleus, made of frozen gases and dust particles; a large coma, also called the head of the comet, made of gas and dust; and a long, sweeping tail of fine particles of dust and gas.

The Nucleus

The nucleus makes up the main part of a comet. It is very compact, at least in space terms—usually no wider than a few miles across. The structure of the nucleus is similar to that of a large, dirty snowball. In other words, it is not very hard or solid. It is solid enough, however, to hold harder particles within its mass. The ingredients of the nucleus are water ice and compounds of hydrogen, carbon, oxygen, and nitrogen. Grains of dust made of minerals called silicates and traces of metals are embedded in this wad of ice. A dark crust covers most of a comet's surface.

When a comet is far from the Sun, the nucleus reflects very little sunlight. But nearer the Sun, a process called resonance fluorescence affects the comet. As a comet gets closer to the Sun, the sunlight's intensity on the nucleus increases. This causes icy material on the surface of the comet to vaporize, and jets of gas and dust spew from the nucleus. These eruptions blend together to form the coma, a glowing halo surrounding the nucleus.

The Coma

Even though there is much less matter contained in the coma than in the nucleus, the coma is much larger. A coma can stretch more than 60,000 miles (96,000 kilometers) wide. An enormous cloud of invisible hydrogen atoms may also surround the visible coma. This cloud may have a diameter of 10 million miles (16 million kilometers.)

The glowing gases of the coma both absorb and reflect sunlight, and the dust in the coma scatters sunlight. This combination makes the brightness of the coma of a comet near the Sun 100 times greater than the light reflected from the nucleus.

The Tail

As the Sun continues to warm a comet, gas molecules (very small particles of matter) are broken down into simpler fragments. Some of these fragments become electrically charged. A combination of the effects of radiation and gravity from the Sun causes the material in the coma to be pushed out in a gently curved tail. Scientists call this the dust tail. Solar wind, fast-moving particles flowing outward from the Sun, may also form an additional tail, which is blue

Comet West, photographed in March 1976, has two tails—a white dust tail and a blue gas tail.

and almost straight. This is called a gas tail.

The solar wind and other Sun-related effects may also cause a comet to send out sharp rays of gas or even to develop two or more tails at the same time. Like a salamander, a comet can lose a tail, then grow a new one. Solar wind can even tie a comet tail into bright knots of light in the sky!

Comet Orbits

Every comet follows a path around the Sun, called an orbit. Comet orbits are always elliptical, or oval, in shape. Some orbits are a little more circular, though, while others are very long and narrow.

The length of time that it takes for a comet to travel its full orbit is called its period. A comet with a more circular orbit is called a short-period comet. This means that it takes fewer years for it to complete its orbit around the Sun. The comet with the shortest known orbital period is Encke's Comet, which reappears punctually every 3.3 years. In contrast, a long-period comet may have an orbit that takes thousands, or even millions, of years to complete.

A comet traveling away from the Sun eventually reaches its aphelion—the most distant point on its orbit. This is when a comet moves most slowly. When a comet comes closest to the Sun, that point is its perihelion. The perihelion of a comet is often not far from the orbit of the Earth. So, because the Sun illuminates a comet, a comet may become visible from Earth. Some comets are so bright that they can be seen in the daytime. The degree of a comet's brightness is called its luminosity.

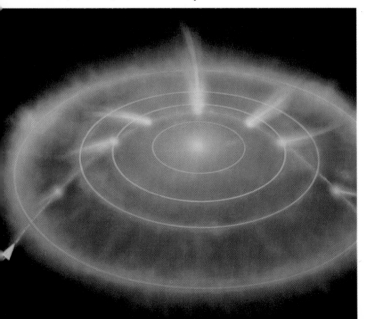

This diagram shows the path of a comet as it rounds the Sun, together with the orbits of Mars, Earth, Venus, and Mercury.

When a comet comes close enough to be detected through a large telescope, it appears to be a faint star. This is often the time when a professional astronomer or an amateur sky-watcher will discover a new comet. How close a comet must come to Earth before we can see it depends on the size of its nucleus. The larger and newer a comet is, the more likely it is that it will be visible from Earth. The smaller and more worn down a comet is from frequent passes by the Sun, the less chance there is that we will catch a glimpse of it.

Professional astronomers usually make their new comet discoveries from photographic plates. These are large pieces of glass or metal used like film. Images that appear on the plate are taken with telescopes that have wide-field lenses, which can capture a large portion of the sky. The astronomers may not even be looking for comets but discover them while doing other types of space research. By taking photographs of part of the sky at set intervals of time, the photographic plates reveal which objects have moved significantly. The objects that move are probably comets. Skilled amateurs usually discover comets by searching the sky with small telescopes. And some comets have been discovered from spacecraft. Six were found during a sky survey made in 1983 by the Infrared Astronomical Satellite (IRAS).

The Naming of Comets

To keep track of all these comets, they are catalogued, or officially recorded, and named. This is done by the Harvard-Smithsonian Center for Astrophysics in Cambridge, Massachusetts, unofficially referred to as Cometsville, USA. Originally, comets were named

Halley's Comet

English astronomer Edmund Halley (rhymes with Sally) was born in 1656. In 1682, Halley saw a bright comet in the sky, and he tried to calculate its orbit. He would work on this puzzling problem for many years.

To help solve the riddle, Halley collected all the information on comets available at the time. By studying these data, he learned that the Comet of 1607 had traveled across the same part of the sky that the Comet of 1682 had.

Next Halley figured out that the Comet of 1531 had done the very same thing. He observed that there had been a lapse of 75 or 76 years between each appearance of these comets. And he concluded that these were not different comets but the very same comet making regular passes through the sky.

Halley did not rush out and announce his astonishing news. The possible loss of position and public ridicule were enough to make most astronomers think twice before sharing radical new information, no matter how exciting or accurate.

By 1705, Halley had all the calculations that he thought he needed to prove that the Comet of 1682 would return in 1758, and he announced his findings. The astronomer would have had to live to be 102 years old to see if his prediction came true. But Halley died in 1742, at age 85.

Even though his forecast caused a temporary sensation, scientists and citizens went on with their lives. Only as time drew closer for the comet's anticipated return did some scientists and amateur astronomers begin to keep their eyes on the sky.

In 1758, Johann Georg Palitzsch, a wealthy German farmer, set up his telescope to watch for the promised return of the apparition. On Christmas, he got a great gift. He was the first person to spy the returning comet!

As the months passed, the comet grew brighter. From this time on, the comet was known as Halley's Comet—or as we are more likely to say today, Comet Halley.

Comet Halley made its faithful reappearance in the years 1835, 1910, and 1986. Perhaps you saw it. If not, be patient: The year 2061 is the next scheduled return of Comet Halley.

for the legendary goddesses from the mythological tales written by ancient Greeks and Romans. Then, as those names ran out, comets were named for girlfriends, wives, mothers, sisters, and any other feminine names that discoverers could think of.

Today, newly discovered comets and returning periodic comets are assigned a temporary name, or designation. This name includes the year of discovery and the order that the comet was discovered in, as indicated by a letter of the alphabet. An example would be 1976 c, for the third comet discovered in 1976.

Once a comet's orbit is established, it is given a permanent name. This name includes the year of discovery plus the order in the year that the comet reaches perihelion. Such a catalogue entry might be 1991 III, meaning a comet discovered in 1991 that was the third comet that year to reach perihelion.

Each newly discovered comet may also be identified by the name (or names, up to three) of its discoverers. This explains a comet that has a name almost as long as its tail, such as Comet Sugano-Saigusa-Fujikawa! Sometimes a comet is not named for its discoverer or discoverers. Instead, it is named for the first person to recognize that a previously observed space body is actually a comet. Comet Encke was named in this way.

From Fear to Understanding

In ancient times, the sudden and unexpected appearance of a comet startled people. Such puzzling and alarming sights were sometimes dismissed as disturbances in the atmosphere. Sometimes they were feared as omens of terrible things to come, such as war or famine.

Comet Fever

A writer once penned this seemingly silly rhyme: "Twinkle, twinkle, little comet/Did you come to make us vomit?" But it's not really silly, for at one time, people believed that comets spewed disease-laden dust upon the Earth. Indeed, comets have been blamed for everything from wars, catastrophic storms, and poor harvests to epidemics of the plague, the murder of Roman military genius Julius Caesar, and almost any other disaster you can think of. Even astronomer Edmund Halley himself once believed that a comet was the cause of the Great Flood mentioned in the Bible.

Most early peoples thought that these mysterious space apparitions were sure signs of trouble. They did not seem to follow any of the rules that guided other heavenly bodies. People insisted that terrible events that occurred after a comet's appearance were proof that comets were evil demons in the sky.

In A.D. 66, Nero, the emperor of Rome, was so afraid that a passing comet meant someone planned to kill him that he struck first: Nero starved or poisoned a number of his subjects. The emperor

Although the appearance of a comet was frightening for most people, even early sky-watchers wondered if they were seeing the same space objects over and over again. Finally, in 1472, two decades before Christopher Columbus sailed on what would become known as his first voyage to the "New World," German astronomer Johannes Muller took a calm, calculated look at comets. He and one of his students did something that no one else had ever done before: They charted the position of a comet against the stars and drew an imaginary line across the sky to indicate the comet's orbit.

survived the comet, then later committed suicide. Yet many Romans still blamed his death on the comet!

A growing number of comets began appearing in the sky, which only increased the panic. Nearly 900 comets were reported during the centuries before the telescope was invented in the 1600s. Between the years 1400 and 1600, there was an unusual abundance of comets.

Entrepreneurs saw opportunity in people's fear. "Comet pills" were sold to ward off any infection from comet dust. You could purchase comet insurance. And coins were minted to be handed out to lucky folks who missed getting conked on the head by a comet.

Some people argued that comets were just ordinary astronomical objects and no reason for fear. A 1686 Dutch comet coin even admitted on its face, "Not All that Terrifies Harms." But few people listened to or believed that "ridiculous" idea for quite a long time. Even as recently as 1970, many Egyptians feared that Comet Bennett was a secret weapon aimed at them by their enemies. And in 1979, there were claims that comets dropped flies, frogs, and animals to Earth.

Not long after that, in 1538, an observant Italian astronomer, Girolamo Fracastoro, noticed that the tail of any comet always pointed away from the Sun. In a 1540 book, Peter Apian, a German astronomer, reported the same conclusion. He drew the first scientific sketch of a comet, with its tail correctly pointing outward from the Sun. Our understanding of comets had begun.

Slowly, early scientists began to learn more about these strange celestial objects. Danish astronomer Tycho Brahe was able to demonstrate that the great comet of 1577 was much farther away from Earth than the Moon was. This was astronomical news, because since the death of the Greek philosopher Aristotle, in 322 B.C., people had generally accepted his belief that comets were flames that were slowly burning in Earth's upper atmosphere.

Like German astronomer Johannes Kepler (1571–1630), most comet-watchers noticed that a comet's orbit did not look anything like the orbit of a planet that circled the Sun. A comet seemed to travel in a straight line. Kepler proposed that comets come into view from a far distance in space and later vanish into space in the opposite direction.

After the Italian scientist Galileo Galilei constructed a simple telescope in 1609, astronomers were able to see comets and other space objects in greater detail. They began to wonder about some of the false assumptions that had been made about comets in the past.

Tycho Brahe discovered that the Comet of 1577 was farther away from the Earth than the Moon was.

Even with the aid of the telescope, however, scientists of the era continued to believe that a comet traveled on a straight path. Giovanni Alfonso Borelli, an Italian scientist, disagreed. He correctly observed that a comet's path around the Sun was not in a straight line, but in the shape of a U.

Otto von Guericke, a German, was the first scientist to conclude that comets did not just pass by the Sun once and then disappear forever. He thought that they must travel on an elliptical orbit—and so eventually return to swing around the Sun once more. Although he was correct, it was not until English scientist Isaac Newton came along that this idea was used to clear up the confusing picture of comets and their orbits.

Newton and the Law of Gravity

After Isaac Newton described his Law of Gravitation (the force of attraction between two objects because of their masses) in 1687, the actions of an orbiting comet were more easily understood. For example, Newton said that a comet could travel around the Sun either in a very long ellipse or in a parabola (an open curve). He could tell one type of orbit from the other by noting the distance of a comet from the Sun and its speed at that distance. If the comet's orbit is an ellipse, the comet will eventually reach the end of its orbit, then turn around, and come back into our solar system and pass the Sun again. If the orbit is a parabola, or open-ended, the celestial body may pass through our solar system once but will keep on going out into space, never to return.

Using his new law, Newton discovered a way to determine a comet's orbit from the part of its path that he could observe from Earth. For example, he figured out that the comet of December 1680 had an orbit that was almost parabolic and he predicted that it would return sometime in the future.

In 1705, English astronomer Edmund Halley described the orbits of 24 comets by using Newton's theories. The sudden, surprising appearance and the seemingly erratic motion of comets were now understood to be a result of the shape of their orbits and the effect of the gravitational pull of the Sun.

Comet Bennett, shown here in false color, was one of the more luminous comets as it passed by the Sun in 1970.

CHAPTER 2

DIRTY SNOWBALLS FROM SPACE

The brightest comets are those making their first pass of the Sun. They are brightest then because they have lost a minimal amount of mass—the material that they are made of—since the Sun has not yet had a chance to melt any of it.

Because we do not yet know their periodicity, their appearance comes as a surprise. Astronomers may spot the faint dot with high-powered telescopes weeks or months before the comet comes close to Earth. Brighter comets can generally be seen with the unaided eye.

Four centuries ago, Johannes Kepler was asked how many comets he thought were in the universe. "As many as there are fish in the sea," he answered. This was an excellent guess, especially considering the fact that only about 900 comets had been documented during his day.

Comets, Artists, and Writers

The dramatic appearance of comets strongly influenced early artists. Comet Halley had a creative impact. After its swing around the Sun in 1066, French artists created the Bayeux Tapestry, a long strip of linen embroidered with 70 scenes of the invasion of England by William of Normandy. The comet was featured prominently in the tapestry, with men pointing to it and (in Latin) the caption: "These wonder at the star."

In 1304, Giotto di Bondone, an Italian artist, created a great painting: *Adoration of the Magi*. This work depicted the Wise Men who came to worship the baby Jesus in his manger in Bethlehem. As in most paintings of this event, the Star in the East that the Wise Men followed is featured. In this work, however, it appears as a comet. It is likely that the artist was influenced by the 1301 appearance of Halley's Comet, which he had witnessed just a couple of years before he began the painting. Many people in those days believed that the Star of Bethlehem had actually been a comet.

Writers were equally in awe of the great comets they witnessed. The English playwright William Shakespeare once wrote that comets indicate "change of times and states." *Cometomania*, a book published in 1684, claimed, "Comets suck the juices from the Earth, so we should expect famine, disease and death." In H. G.

In 1801, Jean Louis Pons was the doorkeeper at the Marseilles Observatory in France when he found his first comet. After being promoted to assistant astronomer, he went on to discover 37 other comets, including, in 1805, the one that would become known as Encke. It was named for Johann Franz Encke, a German astronomer, because he was the first to determine that it was not a new comet but one that had previously visited our

Wells's book *In the Days of the Comet*, gas from a comet's tail caused an outbreak on Earth—but an outbreak of peace and love instead of illness! A 1977 novel, *Lucifer's Hammer*, starred a comet that destroyed civilization with tidal waves and nuclear wars. And in the 1987 science-fiction thriller *Meteor*, a comet smashed into New York City.

One author could not be convinced that a comet's return did not mean personal doom. Mark Twain, the American author of the classics *The Adventures of Tom Sawyer* (1876) and *The Adventures of Huckleberry Finn* (1884), was deathly ill when Comet Halley returned in 1910. Twain had been born 75 years earlier, when that same comet had appeared in the sky. From his deathbed, he predicted to worried onlookers: "I came in with the comet and I shall go out with it." On April 21, the day after Comet Halley passed perihelion, Twain died.

The drama and beauty of comets have inspired artists and writers throughout history.

solar system. He calculated that the very short-period comet circled the Sun every 3.3 years. Encke also calculated the orbits of at least 56 other comets. What once had seemed impossible was now routine.

Using today's powerful telescopes, a new comet is spotted on the average of every two to three weeks. And these, scientists believe, are just a small fraction of the comets that may exist.

Comet Kohoutek's tail shows evidence of dust, oxygen, and other gases in this false-color photo taken by *Skylab 4*.

It is always a major astronomical event when a long-period comet makes its appearance. Comet Kohoutek did this in 1973 to 1974. Lubos Kohoutek, for whom the comet is named, detected the comet while it was still far beyond the planet Jupiter. Kohoutek tracked the comet from the time he first saw it until it passed the Sun and then receded deep into space. Because so much of the comet's path could be calculated, scientists used that information to determine the rest of the comet's orbit—the largest ever plotted for any body in the solar system. They found that the comet would not be seen again for up to 80,000 years!

Because of the Sun's powerful gravitational pull, scientists expect to discover comets with even longer periods, which may have been traveling in space for many, many years and only now come into view. The discovery of Comet Hyakutake early in 1996 is an example. This comet has a periodicity of around 18,000 years. In its first pass by the Sun in 1996, it was easy to see from Earth, even without the aid of a telescope.

The Century of Comets

Since they orbit the Sun so infrequently, long-period comets lose very little of their substance to the strong gravitational pull of the star. Thus, they often develop large comas and long tails, because they have more matter to give off than comets that have passed the Sun many times.

The nineteenth century was marked by a blaze of brilliant comets. In 1811, an enormous comet appeared. Its tail grew to the spectacular length of 100 million miles (161 million kilometers)—longer than the distance from the Earth to the Sun. Visible from Earth through a telescope for 1 1/2 years, the Comet of 1811 was an especially dramatic sight. It could be seen with only the naked eye for several weeks.

The Great March Comet of 1843 passed a mere 80,000 miles (128,744 kilometers) from the surface of the Sun. This "Sun-grazer" spewed its tail over one-fourth of the sky, as viewed from Earth. Moving at 350 miles (563 kilometers) per second, it passed three-fourths of the way around the Sun in just half a day.

In 1858, the third new comet of the century, Donati, was a crowd-pleaser, spouting several tails that changed in shape. This happens because, as the Sun heats a comet, ice enclosed in the nucleus may evaporate. The accumulated vapor blows rocky material away in an explosion, causing changes in the shape of the coma and tail. Acting like rockets, these explosions can push a comet forward, backward, or sideways. (Astronomers had long wondered why comets sometimes seemed to move erratically on their orbits, and this discovery helped to explain the phenomenon.) The number of bobbling detours that a comet

Carolyn Shoemaker and Other Women Astronomers

By 1961, when scientist Carolyn Shoemaker was only 32 years old, she had discovered more comets than any other living person. Shoemaker is just one of many women astronomers whose distinguished careers are inspiring other people to join them in this fascinating field.

In 1994, a comet named Shoemaker-Levy 9 was on course to collide with the planet Jupiter. The comet, discovered in 1993, was named for co-discoverers Carolyn and Gene Shoemaker and David Levy. Astronomers were excited about the forthcoming slam-dunk of a comet into a planet, something that had never been witnessed before.

Many of the astronomers were women, professionals in a variety of space-science fields. Heidi Hammel was responsible for making sure that NASA's Hubble Space Telescope took photographs of the event. She also set up a network of observatories around the world to track the progress of the comet. A professor of astronomy at the University of California at Berkeley, Imke de Pater, used the world's largest optical telescope, located at the Keck Observatory in Hawaii, to observe the event. Lucy McFadden, a visiting professor of astronomy at the University of Maryland, also helped to coordinate a worldwide study of the comet's crash. Reta Beebe, a professor of astronomy at New Mexico State University, who had studied planets for 25 years, was shocked to see the impact that such a small comet could have on a large planet like Jupiter.

Carolyn Shoemaker

Many people—including these boaters—gathered to watch Comet Donati during the fall of 1858.

takes affects the time it takes it to reach perihelion, since these additional movements can throw the comet off its orbit slightly.

Giovanni Battista Donati, the Italian astronomer who discovered the 1858 comet, was also the first to analyze the wavelengths of light (or light spectrum) of a comet. The lines and bands found in a comet's light spectrum actually represent various types of matter. By analyzing this "spectral pattern" of a particular comet, scientists can learn what type of materials that comet is made of. Dark lines, where no light is reflected, indicate that substances around the comet have absorbed light. By analyzing the position of the dark lines in the spectrum of Comet

Donati, English astronomer William Huggins was able to identify some of the substances in the coma in 1868. This became a cornerstone for study of cometary composition. Such analyses have proved that comets are mainly made up of water molecules.

Australians were the first to spot a new comet in 1861, but they had no quick way to communicate the exciting news to the rest of the world; it was passed along slowly, by ship. Since word of the approaching comet was not received beforehand, Europeans and Americans were surprised by the large, bright comet. It came especially close to Earth for a comet, only 11 million miles (17.7 million kilometers) away. Some observers in the United States claimed that the comet was a warning from God of the many deaths that would occur during the Civil War, which erupted that year on American soil.

The Comet of 1882 was the first to have a good-quality photograph taken of it. This was the beginning of the discovery of comets through the use of photography, as opposed to the use of the naked eye.

The Birth of a Comet

By the late 1800s, astronomers suspected that, following the birth of the solar system, massive numbers of comets were formed in the outer part of the solar nebula—the cloud of dust and gas from which the Sun, planets, and other bodies of the solar system are believed to have formed around 4.6 billion years ago. This means that the comets would have formed near the most distant planets, or even much deeper in space. They further thought that, following the initial explosion (known as the Big Bang) that is believed to have created the universe, some solid grains of material condensed in interstellar clouds. Because some of this material exists in a comet's nucleus, remaining almost unchanged since the beginning of the universe, scientists study these "time capsules" to learn how the universe began and grew.

It was not until 1950 that a Dutch astronomer named Jan Hendrik Oort figured out where comets were born. Oort studied the sizes and shapes of the most stable comet orbits known. He concluded that fresh comets must come from some large "comet warehouse" in the far reaches of space. This "storage cloud" of comets would come to be known as the Oort Cloud. Oort estimated that this storage cloud in space might hold 100 billion comets. (Scientists today believe that there are probably many more comets than this, both in the Oort Cloud and in a closer location, called the Kuiper Belt.)

Within the Oort Cloud, deep in space, comets move slowly as they are continually stirred by the gravitational pull of passing stars. Occasionally, these gravitational forces pull a comet into orbit, where it will sooner or later be drawn around the Sun and become visible on Earth.

Death of a Comet

After a comet's orbit takes it past the Sun, it may return to the Oort Cloud. However, a comet can be shoved into interstellar space on an orbit that will not bring it past the Sun again. Some comets end their lives by plunging directly into the Sun itself.

Even a comet with a large nucleus of ice will eventually melt. When a comet is new, its mass is the most solid and frozen that it will ever be, and the comet gives off its brightest light as it passes the Sun. With each orbit, the Sun's heat and gravity tug at the passing comet, causing it to grow smaller through the loss of material given off as gases and streams of dust. After a few hundred or thousand revolutions, the ice ball disintegrates.

As a comet dies, it slowly breaks apart, leaving debris. Some of the debris may form meteroids. The comet continues to travel in its orbit along with the meteoroids that it creates. The nucleus can also become so covered with matter that the gas and dust within can no longer escape to form a coma or tail.

The Oort Cloud—shown here in an artist's representation—is the birthplace of many comets. (The Sun is shown upper right.)

The Kuiper Belt

Even though the discovery of the Oort Cloud helped to answer where comets come from, scientists felt sure that there was a "comet home" closer than the far reaches of space. This home, first proposed to exist in 1950, is the Kuiper Belt. It was difficult for astronomers to find, though there are millions of bits of space matter there, since the pieces are not large enough to be easily located with Earth-based telescopes. But scientists had become curious about a spot in space that seemed to be empty. When they investigated, they found that it is filled with hundreds of millions of comets!

In 1987, astronomers Jane Luu and David Jewett teamed up to find this disk-shaped mass of comets. They had to struggle to get telescope time for a project that some people considered hopeless. Luu and Jewett described their search as "... looking for something the size of Manhattan and the color of coal from 4 billion miles away." But these patient sky-watchers were credited with discovering the location of the Kuiper Belt.

It begins just outside of the orbit of the planet Neptune and extends to a place a few hundred times Earth's distance from the Sun. Scientists believe that this is the source of the about 150 short-period comets that orbit the Sun every 20 years or less. Now all astronomers are eager to study these "giants preserved in ice" to see what they say about the birth of our solar system.

A comet's nucleus may erupt, causing the comet to vanish, except for a swarm of particles that follow the orbit like sparkling dust. When a comet's gas and dust are exhausted or are trapped within the nucleus and unable to escape, the comet is called inactive.

A meteor, photographed here during a display of the northern lights, can be seen falling from the center to the bottom right.

CHAPTER 3

MIGHTY METEORS

Space is filled with objects of all sizes. These bodies are all called different things, depending on where they are located at a particular time and what they are doing.

A meteoroid is a solid object that is either located in interplanetary space or is passing through Earth's atmosphere. While scientists still do not completely understand the origin of meteoroids, they believe that they are formed from "parent comets."

Some meteoroids fall into Earth's atmosphere. This collision between the meteoroid and the atmosphere is called a meteor. The term *meteor* comes from two Greek words meaning "thing in the heavens above" and "high in the air." It is used today to indicate the streak of light seen in the night sky when an object from space enters Earth's atmosphere. Meteors are more commonly called either falling stars or shooting stars.

Large meteors may not completely vaporize as they tumble through Earth's atmosphere; the unvaporized particles that eventually fall to Earth's surface are called meteorites. Their impact with Earth can create craters on the surface of the planet.

Scientists analyze the light that meteors produce as they vaporize to learn about them. This light is produced by the collision of the meteor with air particles. In the process, some atoms are torn from the meteoroid. These atoms evaporate, which causes the air particles to radiate light for an instant. How much light a meteor gives off is determined by the amount of matter that disintegrates during its fall through the atmosphere.

Fireballs and Micrometeorites

A very large, bright meteor is often called a fireball. One can give off more light than the full Moon, at least for a few seconds; sometimes fireballs appear to be even brighter than the Moon. Shock waves, created by the collision of air particles, often follow the appearance of a fireball. The ground may shake, and windows can rattle or even break. A fireball that explodes in the atmosphere is called a bolide.

On August 4, 1835, around 4:30 P.M., residents of Aldsworth, England, heard a loud boom. In the sky, some spotted a copper-colored fireball that had a tail. A meteorite fell very near some workmen in a field. More than 875 miles (1,408 kilometers) south, children stuck out their hands to catch the surprising shower of "black beetles" (as they mistakenly described them) that rained down upon them, as part of this same event. The fallen meteorite weighed only 21 ounces (595 grams) and was about 4 inches (10 centimeters) across.

The famous 1908 Tunguska Fireball in Siberia exploded in the atmosphere, close to the ground. It produced no crater.

The 1933 Pasamonte meteorite, seen by people in New Mexico, Colorado, Kansas, Oklahoma, and Texas, left a twisting dust trail of superfine particles. This indicated that the fireball had fallen in a spiral path. The largest known meteorite fell in 1976, when a bright fireball was spotted and 4.5 tons (4 metric tons) of space debris pummeled Jilin, China. The largest piece recovered was a 2-ton (1.8-metric-ton) whopper.

Humming or whistling sounds often accompany the fall of meteorites. In 1991, a British gardener was shocked to hear a whine and see an object crash through a nearby hedge. He soon recovered a 27-ounce (765-gram) meteorite—still warm to the touch from its blisteringly fast fall through the atmosphere.

Dust-sized particles of interplanetary matter can filter through the atmosphere, with or without melting. These objects are called micrometeorites. The term *micrometeorites* is also used for any small fragment from the disintegration of a larger space object that makes its way to Earth and is recovered.

Paths and Radiants

If you go outside on a clear night, with little light to distort your vision, you might see a meteor streak by in the sky. Don't blink! Most last only half a second, with one to two seconds about the longest amount of time that a meteor is visible.

The best time to spot meteors is usually just after midnight. Obviously, some nights are better than others for sighting these "falling stars." Since most meteors give off a faint light, it is best to watch for them from a place where the sky can be seen at its darkest, such as away from city lights.

How far away are meteors that look like they could fall into your lap? That can be tricky to determine. The direction that the brief streak of light takes against the backdrop of the stars is called the apparent path of the meteor. The stars are much farther away than the meteor, but they give you a measuring stick to calculate the meteor's approximate distance from Earth.

If you see a meteor and note its path in the sky, according to the stars, and your friend who lives several miles away sees the same meteor and records the path, you will discover that the paths you observed vary just a little. By determining the difference between the paths—the parallax—you can determine how far away the meteor was when it entered the atmosphere. It is very hard to do this from what you see with the unaided eye. Photography, however, can catch this action and provide a more accurate measurement to obtain the distance the meteor was from Earth.

Most meteors start out 40 to 70 miles (64 to 112 kilometers) above the Earth's surface. They vanish from sight about 15 miles (24 kilometers) below the point at which they first appeared in the sky. The speed of a meteor's fall can be determined with a camera. This is done by photographing the beam of light at equal time intervals, such as 20 or 30 times a second. This will produce a photographic trail, a series of segments from which the meteor's speed can be calculated.

You may describe the meteor you saw as having an arc-shaped path. Your friend might disagree, insisting that she saw an almost straight path, or even that the meteor seemed to be more of a point of light heading directly toward her. But both of you are correct, because the apparent path of the meteor depends on the location from which it is seen.

The location of the point in the sky that the meteor seems to come from is called the radiant. All the other paths that the meteor appears to take radiate away from this point. The actual path of a meteor is a straight line.

Shooting Stars

Meteors travel in an orbit called an ellipse, just as comets do. Some orbits may be eccentric. This term indicates how stretched out the ellipsis is. Some meteor orbits are quite eccentric, shaped more like a long, skinny surfboard than the near-circle of a less eccentric meteor orbit.

The orbit of a meteoroid that is part of a meteor shower is similar to the orbit of its parent comet. Because the comet has already come and gone—leaving debris behind it, which spreads out in the wake of its orbit—it is possible only about half the time for astronomers to match the meteoroid with the comet that created it. This is because the meteor stream gets dispersed over time.

In addition, the orbit changes slightly. Meteors that have gotten out of this orbital mainstream and appear randomly are called sporadic meteors. These include meteors that are created during a collision between asteroids.

Astronomers use visual observations to collect statistical data about meteors. But they must rely on special cameras that can photograph a large portion of space to measure their brightness and speed accurately. As early as the 1930s, radar, which was used by the military, was also used as a main way to observe meteors. In this method, a radar transmitter sends out an electronic beam in a series of short pulses. While a meteoroid is too small to be the target of these so-called radio waves, the collision between the meteoroid and Earth's atmosphere can reflect the radar beam. Since radar can operate in daylight and through clouds, meteor activity can be measured around the clock.

Meteor Showers

Because astronomers can determine approximately when comets will return on their orbits around the Sun, they can also forecast meteor showers. A meteor shower is named for occasional short terms of intense meteor activity, during which meteors are so frequent that they seem to rain from the sky. For centuries, people have marveled at these events.

Meteor showers are named for the point, or radiant, in the sky from which they appear to come. The Leonid shower, usually a modest rain of meteors that lasts for a couple of days, is named for the constellation Leo, its apparent source. The shower can also be named for a particular star that is located near the radiant.

Annual predictions of meteor showers can be made because small, solid particles, released from the nucleus of a comet by solar heating when it comes close to the Sun, survive to travel in the comet's orbit. After a few centuries, these comet "crumbs" become distributed around the entire orbit. If the material is fairly evenly spread out and Earth crosses this comet path at least once a year, then an annual meteor shower can reliably be forecast.

Even though the meteors in a shower can be all sizes and shapes, they still appear to be roughly the same size and to come from the same direction, depending upon the viewer's location. The number of meteors in a shower is less predictable. The Leonid shower gave off great displays in 1833, 1866, and 1966. Observers could see 2,000 to 5,000 meteors in a single hour in 1866 and 60,000 per hour during the peak times in 1966. In

The annual Leonid meteor shower, photographed here in false color on November 17, 1966, showered a record 40,000 meteors in 40 minutes.

1833, when a shower of 200,000 meteors flooded Earth's sky, many people believed that the end of the world had come!

New meteor showers can appear at any time that material released from a long-period comet makes its first passage through the inner solar system. Meteors near the Earth travel as fast as 45 miles (72 kilometers) per second. Others travel as slow as 14 miles (22 kilometers) per second.

Luminous Logic

The amount of light that a meteor gives off is related to the mass of the particle that is vaporized during collision with Earth's atmosphere. A meteor with a peak brightness equal to the brightest stars in the sky requires a particle of about 1/28 ounce (1 gram) in mass. Very faint meteors may have a mass 100 times less than this. Radar can detect a meteor with a mass even 1,000 times less than the brightest meteor. A fireball meteor as bright as the Moon may have a mass of several pounds.

Meteorites: Messengers from Space

Before astronauts brought rock samples back from the Moon, meteorites were the only material from space that scientists had to study in the laboratory. It takes several pounds of meteor, entering the upper atmosphere at a minimum speed of 7 miles (11 kilometers) per second, to land a meteorite on Earth.

When eyewitnesses confirm a meteorite impact, it is called a fall. When a meteorite is discovered but the time of its fall is unknown, it is called a find. Meteorites are usually named after a nearby town or for a nearby river, lake, or other geographic feature. If many pieces fall, they all have the same name.

Falls and Finds

A scientific catalogue of all known meteorites includes more than 3,000 entries. The size and recovered masses range from 1/200 ounce (0.14 gram) for a meteorite found in Canada in a 1967 fall to a 60-ton (55-metric-ton) estimate for a giant meteorite named Hoba, which fell in Namibia in southern Africa at some unknown time in the past. This whopper meteorite, discovered around 1920, is about 10 feet (3 meters) across and 3 feet (1 meter) thick.

The Hoba meteorite, which fell on Namibia, is thought to be the largest one on Earth.

While many ancient reports of falling stars probably were of meteorites, some may have been hailstones. The oldest meteorite fall ever seen, where specimens were recovered and are still preserved, was in eastern France in 1492. But it was not until the 1833 Leonid shower that scientists were convinced that meteorites really were falling from the sky. Networks of cameras set up in the prairie states of the United States and in Canada have managed to capture pictures of meteorites in the act of falling. More than 100 meteorites have been found in just one area of New Mexico. Archaeologists have unearthed meteorites in ancient Indian burial mounds, suggesting that these early peoples revered the fallen objects.

In Antarctica in 1969, some Japanese workers found nine meteorites. In the 1970s, Japanese and American workers collected almost 5,000 meteorite samples there. The discoveries were made after glacial ice melt and high winds exposed some of the meteorites. The Antarctic Search for Meteorites (Ansmet) program continues to pile up meteorites from this frozen continent.

Usually, 12 to 24 meteorites are recovered throughout the world over the course of a year. However, many years can pass between the time that a meteorite is found and the time that it is reported. This is especially true if the finder is in a remote area of the world or tucks it away, thinking it is merely an unusual-looking rock. Scientists suspect that there are around 500 meteorite-dropping events each year. The daily total mass of the meteorite falls is estimated at approximately 1,000 tons (907 metric tons) for the entire surface of Earth, including bodies of water.

Types of Meteorites

There are three main types of meteorite: iron, stone, and stony iron. Iron meteorites are also called siderites. Primarily made of iron and some nickel, irons are around eight times as heavy as water. Usually dark and rusty looking, they may have thumb-print-like impressions on their surface, caused by uneven burning off of the outer layers during their pass through the atmosphere. Farmers often find irons in fields, which they identify by their look and the metallic ring they give off when struck by a metal object such as a shovel. And they were also found by prehistoric peoples, who used them as rough forms of tools, perhaps for digging, carving, or hammering.

Stone meteorites, which are called aerolites, account for more than 90 percent of the meteorites that fall to Earth. They may have a thin, black crust. This crust may weather away after they fall, leaving them unrecognizable as meteorites. Since stone meteorites that survive their trip through the atmosphere usually break into pieces upon their impact with the ground, they generally have a flat side with sharp edges. This type of meteorite is also called a chondrite, named for the chondrules, or small pieces of rock, that they may contain. The insides of these rocks are white, brown, gray, or black in color. They are more than three times as hard as water, and they are much harder than the average rock. Meteorites called anchondrites do not contain these rocks.

Carbonaceous chondrites are a rare type of stone meteorite. They are important because they are the oldest material that exists on Earth. Since they are so fragile, little of their mass

Those Crash Sites: The Craters

Astronomers agree that the heavy bombardment of the solar system with meteorites ended about 3 billion years ago, leaving the Moon, the planets Mars and Mercury, Jupiter's moons, and other space objects deeply pitted. Since then, such impacts have been steady but fewer. A few new craters 1 mile (1.6 kilometers) or more in diameter are still formed on Earth every million years.

The Arizona Crater (also called Meteor Crater or Barringer Crater) was blasted into the Earth between 25,000 and 50,000 years ago. It is three-fourths of a mile (1.2 kilometers) in diameter, with a rim 200 feet (60 meters) above and a floor 650 feet (200 meters) below the surrounding surface. The site of pioneer studies on meteorite impact, this crater has also served as an astronaut training location. This was the first impact site of a celestial body to be identified on Earth. It was probably created by a meteoroid that weighed 69,300 tons (63,000 metric tons) and sped to Earth at 5 to 10 miles (8 to 16 kilometers) per second. Its impact released energy equal to 3.5 tons (3 metric tons) of dynamite. Most of the meteorite vaporized, but around 30 tons (27 metric tons) of fragments that survived have been collected.

In 1947, the Sikhote-Alin Meteorite crashed into eastern Siberia, where around 100 tons (91 metric tons) of iron gouged many pits and craters into the Earth.

survives passage through the atmosphere, making them rare in meteorite collections.

Stony-iron meteorites are also rare, making up only about 1 percent of all observed falls. They consist primarily of equal parts stony material and nickel-iron metal and silicates and are roughly six times as heavy as water.

Meteoritic Impact

As a meteorite passes through the atmosphere, it is slowed by drag effects. At about 12 miles (19 kilometers) above the Earth, a meteorite ceases to produce light and falls as a dark object.

The impact of a meteorite on Earth can be devastating. A large meteorite that falls in the ocean can create tidal waves. Meteorites that hit land blast out craters.

When a large meteorite collides with the Earth, tremendous shock waves are created. These may produce a shatter cone, a type of rock fracture. A meteorite usually is buried in the rock twice as deep as its diameter. But because of the great energy given off at impact, most of the meteorite is vaporized, spewing leftover pieces often far beyond the crater edge. To date, 36 ancient meteor craters have been identified in North America, out of a total of more than 100 in the world.

This painting illustrates an impact with Earth by an object 500 miles (805 kilometers) in diameter.

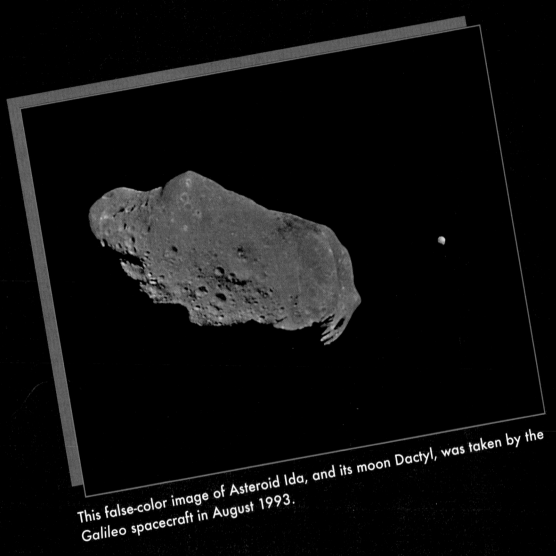

This false-color image of Asteroid Ida, and its moon Dactyl, was taken by the
Galileo spacecraft in August 1993.

CHAPTER 4

ASTEROIDS, THE GODDESSES OF SPACE

An asteroid is a "close relative" of the meteor. It is one of many small "minor planets," or planetoids, that orbit the Sun somewhat like flying mountains. The word *asteroid* means "star like."

In the late 1700s, scientists found themselves in search of a missing planet. After Johannes Kepler had determined the relative distances of the planets from the Sun, scientists noticed that there was an odd gap between Mars and Jupiter. They were excited when the discovery of the asteroid belt filled this void. But while searching for the missing planet, the researchers discovered a number of unexpected objects.

On January 1, 1801, Giuseppe Piazzi, an Italian, began watching a "star" that he suspected was some odd type of comet. He called it Ceres. The scientific world was startled when, in 1802, Heinrick W. M. Olbers, a German astronomer, discovered another strange object, which he named Pallas. Soon astronomers were scrambling to discover these "asteroids." In 1804, German astronomer Karl Harding found Juno, then three years later, Vesta. It was 1845 before a fifth asteroid, Astrea, was observed by Karl Hencke, an amateur astronomer in Germany. Three more asteroids were discovered in 1847, and new ones were spotted each year thereafter.

In the last decade of the 1800s, celestial photography became more advanced. Telescopes with cameras attached could be used to spot dots on photographic plates that had moved, possibly indicating new asteroids.

The Naming of Asteroids

Asteroids are initially named for the year in which they are discovered plus two capital letters, such as 1932 HA. Once an asteroid's orbit is calculated, it is given a permanent number. The early asteroids were named for mythological female goddesses, as comets were. But as astronomers continued to discover so many new asteroids, they resorted to city and country names. Today, there are so many known asteroids that most are represented only by their number, although the discoverer is entitled to name the asteroid anything he or she pleases.

Asteroid Orbits

Only the diameters of the largest asteroids can be measured. From 1894 to 1895, Edward E. Barnard from Tennessee used a large telescope to determine the sizes of the asteroids Ceres, Pallas, Vesta, and Juno. Their sizes ranged between 152 miles

What Happened to the Dinosaurs?

Dinosaurs, the prehistoric creatures that once dominated Earth, were probably unconcerned about space. Perhaps they should have been. While we do not know for sure what caused the dinosaurs to disappear suddenly about 65 million years ago, scientists have suggested one theory.

Archaeological and geological records indicate that a major natural catastrophe occurred on Earth around 65 million years ago. This extraordinary event—whatever it was—may have killed about 90 percent of the animal life that existed on the planet at that time—including the mammoth dinosaurs. For years, scientists have searched for clues as to what this terrible disaster could have been.

Scientists discovered that, almost exactly at the time the dinosaurs became extinct, there was a sudden increase in the amount of a certain element, iridium, on Earth. Iridium is very rare on Earth, but it is quite common elsewhere in the solar system. This made scientists suspect that perhaps the collision with Earth of a body from space, such as a large comet, meteroid, or asteroid, was responsible for an environmental catastrophe on the planet.

An asteroid would have mostly vaporized during its crash through Earth's atmosphere. Because such an asteroid was probably very large in size—with a diameter of at least 6.2 miles (10 kilometers)—it would have spread a dense cloud of dust particles, including iridium, around the planet. If this thick cloud of dust blocked sunlight from reaching Earth, plants would not be able to survive—and, naturally, neither would the animals that depended on the plants for food, including the dinosaurs.

Although there is no way to completely prove this theory at this time, you have only to look at the enormous craters on the Moon and Mars to see what can happen when an especially large asteroid crashes into another celestial body. This theory is now generally accepted because of the existence of a worldwide layer of sediment—discovered in 1980—deposited by the dust cloud and because of the presence of iridium in the sediment.

(244 kilometers) and 584 miles (940 kilometers). Asteroids much smaller than this are generally too small to have their diameter easily determined from such a great distance.

Most asteroids are irregular in shape. Also, since the average asteroid has such a small mass, it cannot have very much gravitational pull. Since asteroids don't have enough gravity to hold an atmosphere around them, they cannot host any type of life.

One artist's impression, resembling a peanut, of Hektor—the largest of the Trojan group of asteroids, at 185 miles (298 kilometers) long.

Collision Course!

While science-fiction movies often depict horror stories of giant asteroids looming over Earth's panicked citizens, we really don't have too much to worry about. However, in 1972, a fragment of an asteroid entered Earth's atmosphere over the state of Idaho. Fortunately, that fragment, which was as big as a house, slipped back into the atmosphere and out into space. But it came within 36 miles (58 kilometers) of the ground, and its 1 million pounds (0.45 million kilograms) traveled 915 miles (1,473 kilometers) before it passed Earth by.

Other asteroids that have come close to our planet are Icarus and Eros, at a few million miles away each, and smaller asteroids such as Hermes, at around 497,111 miles (800,000 kilometers) away. Apollo asteroid number 4581 (also called Asclepius) passed within 434,972 miles (700,000 kilometers) of Earth in 1989. This was the closest recent encounter that we have had with such a celestial object. Many scientists admit that there is a possibility of an Earth/asteroid collision occurring one day.

With enough prior warning, however, many scientists do believe that there might be a way to deflect a space body on a collision course with Earth, should it become necessary.

Asteroids travel in a counter-clockwise orbit around the Sun. While most asteroids roam between the orbits of Jupiter and Mars, there are other asteroid zones. The orbits of most asteroids are like those of the planets, more or less circular. But some asteroids have highly eccentric orbits, like those of comets. It is possible that such asteroids and comets are related, with the asteroid being the nucleus of a comet whose coma has disappeared. Indeed, a comet that no longer glows may be mistaken for an asteroid.

Asteroid Homes

Scientists are still working to learn the origin of asteroids. Asteroids that may have formed from the eruption of the same celestial body are referred to as "families." The breakup of a planet, for instance, could happen through explosion, rapid rotation, tidal disruption, or collision. Dutch-American astronomer Gerard Kuiper developed a theory that states that a number of collisions may have taken place in the universe in the past, allowing many chances for the fragments to bump into one another. This bumper-car theory may explain the irregularity of the shape and size of asteroids as well as the variety of their orbits.

Some astronomers doubt that an exploded planet created the asteroids. It is more likely, they believe, that when the major planets were accumulating during the birth of the solar system, there just wasn't enough space stuff to go around to form another large planet between Jupiter and Mars, especially not with Jupiter's strong gravity tugging on the leftover pieces.

More than 5,000 asteroids are now known, most of them swarming in what is called the asteroid belt. This region lies between Mars and Jupiter. Asteroids located in this area of space orbit the Sun every 3.3 to 6 years. These include a number of asteroid family groups, such as 38 to 45 Amor asteroids, around 700 Apollo asteroids, and about six Aten asteroids. There are 96 Trojans, named for ancient Greek heroes of the Trojan War. The orbits of more than 1,600 asteroids have been calculated. The 100 or so asteroids that cross the Earth's orbit are known as Earth-crossing asteroids. They are of special interest

This artist's impression shows the *Galileo* traveling past Io, one of Jupiter's moons. The satellites of Jupiter may actually be asteroids pulled into the planet's orbit.

to scientists since they may be close enough for us to visit one day, possibly to mine for minerals for use back on Earth.

In 1995, the spacecraft *Galileo* neared Jupiter after traveling since 1989. On July 13, *Galileo* released a probe that explored Jupiter's atmosphere more closely than the main spacecraft could. The *Galileo* mission observed two asteroids, Gaspra and Ida. Both had craters caused by collisions with other asteroids. In fact, Jupiter's gravity has snagged 16 moons, possibly all asteroids. It is also possible that Phobos and Deimos, the two moons of Mars, could be asteroids that the planet's gravity pulled into orbit.

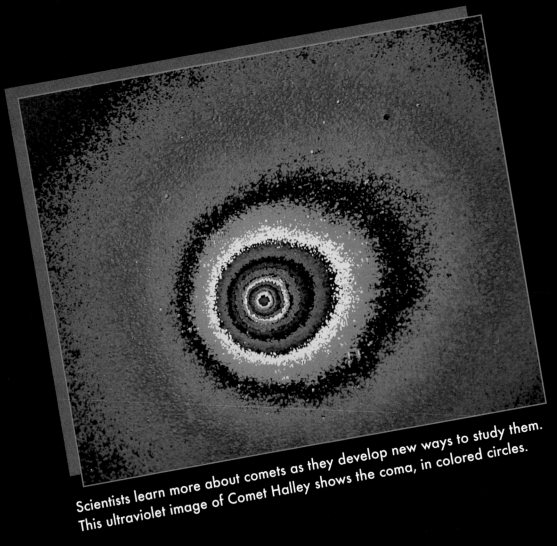
Scientists learn more about comets as they develop new ways to study them. This ultraviolet image of Comet Halley shows the coma, in colored circles.

CHAPTER 5

MESSENGERS FROM THE PAST: COMETS, METEORS, AND ASTEROIDS

It is becoming very clear to scientists that increased knowledge about space objects as old as time—comets, meteors, and asteroids—is offering exciting new answers to our many ongoing questions about the universe. Scientists believe that our solar system formed from a single contracting cloud of gases, the solar nebula. Since space bodies such as comets, meteors, and asteroids probably originated during this event, scientists study them to learn more about how the universe began and developed.

New and improved space-observing tools and technologies add to our knowledge daily. The European Space Agency's *Giotto* spacecraft brought back dramatic and informative photographs of Halley's Comet in 1986. In 1991, the *Galileo* space probe took the first close-up photograph of an asteroid, Gaspra.

Charles Messier: Serious Sky Watcher

Even in his own day, French astronomer Charles Messier was known as a man who discovered comets. Messier was born in Badonviller, France, on June 26, 1730. Between 1759 and 1798, he discovered 15 comets.

But Messier is remembered more for the catalogue of celestial bodies that he created. This catalogue of known space objects such as star clusters and galaxies helped astronomers not to confuse them with the new comets that they were so eagerly searching for. Messier published a final list of 103 items in 1784. (With improved telescopes and methods, English astronomer William Herschel was able to add another 2,500 items to the list by 1803.) Messier died in Paris in 1817, but his catalogue lives on as a valuable aid to the astronomers of today.

The picture showed the asteroid to look like a giant arrowhead hurling through space. NASA's International Cometary Explorer, or *Ice*, spacecraft, launched in 1978, is equipped to study comets and other space bodies.

Scientists have found many reasons to increase their study of asteroids. Asteroids are useful to astronomers as reference points in space—that is, their locations help scientists determine more precisely the location of other celestial bodies. Also, asteroids have been used to make more careful measurements of the solar parallax and the astronomical unit, which scientists use to explain distances in space (one AU equals 92,955,730 miles [149,597,870 kilometers]). A number of observatories around the world are making extensive studies of asteroids.

Pointers to the Future

In 1999, NASA will launch the spacecraft *Stardust*. This space age "dust-buster" will travel through the tail of Comet Wild-2 and actually scoop up some of its cometary material. These comet "crumbs" will be returned to Earth in 2006 for further study. Perhaps this material will prove or disprove the recurring theory that lifeforms on Earth had their beginnings when bacteria fell from the tail of a comet onto the planet.

Some scientists have proposed literally planting comets with tree seeds to create planetlike islands for use as space stations. Others have recommended launching space "tugboats" to snare comets into orbit around Earth so that they can be mined for minerals and metals.

Many scientists have thought about the possibility that life exists in meteorites. Meteorites do contain many of the chemicals needed for the development of some type of lifeform. But it is doubtful whether any meteorites developed all the essential ingredients for life formation. For example, they may never have formed an atmosphere or warmed to the necessary temperature range at which life could form. Only continued studies can help us to

This Martian meteorite found in Antarctica may help scientists gain knowledge about the red planet.

discover whether or not any meteorites attained all of the elements necessary at the same time to allow for the creation of life.

Since life on Mars has not yet been completely disproved, scientists are keeping a close eye on rocks from the red planet. They hope that a future space probe will retrieve samples of Martian soil for examination. Meteorite researchers are also interested in investigating three stone meteorites plucked from the ice-capped Queen Alexandra Range in Antarctica near the end of 1995. It is believed that they could be from the Moon and Mars. There have only been 15 lunar and 12 Martian meteorites retrieved on Earth to date.

Keep Your Eyes on the Sky

In 1839, French author Gustave Flaubert described comets as "running like horses in the field of space." Today, scientists are making galloping gains in knowledge about comets, meteors, and asteroids in the race to better understand our universe.

The study of comets, meteors, and asteroids is an ongoing adventure, for professional and amateur astronomers alike. Although there are larger and more spectacular celestial bodies, even a small chunk of space rock may eventually prove to be the key that unlocks the door to the secrets of space.

For these reasons—as well as for the beauty, wonder, and joy that they bring to us on Earth—keep your eyes on the ever-surprising sky, in search of comets, meteors, and asteroids.

GLOSSARY

....

aphelion The point in a comet's orbit when it is farthest from the Sun.

asteroids Small, solid objects, made of rock or metal, that orbit the Sun.

asteroid belt The region in space between Mars and Jupiter that contains thousands of asteroids.

astronomical unit A unit of measure based on the distance from the Earth to the Sun, or 92,955,730 miles (149,597,870 kilometers).

atmosphere The mass of air that surrounds the Earth.

bolide A fireball that explodes in the atmosphere.

celestial Pertaining to the sky or heavens.

coma The halo-shaped mass of gas and dust that surrounds the nucleus of a comet.

comet A space object of frozen ice that develops a luminous halo and tail when its orbit comes near the Sun.

element A chemical substance that cannot be broken down any further. Some elements are found in nature; others are made in the laboratory. Oxygen and carbon are examples of elements.

fireball A very large, bright meteor.

fluorescence The absorption of sunlight by a comet. The comet then re-radiates the energy.

galaxy A large group of stars, gas, and dust; Earth is in the Milky Way galaxy.

gravity The force of attraction that exists between two objects because of their masses.

grazers Celestial objects that pass close to one another. Sun-grazers are comets that come near the Sun; asteroids that pass near the Earth are Earth-grazers.

interplanetary Existing or occurring between the planets.

interstellar Located between or among the stars.

ionize To be changed into atoms or molecules with a certain type of electric charge.

long period A term for a comet with an orbit that circles the Sun every 200 years or more.

luminosity The degree of light that an object gives off.

mass A unified body of matter that has no specific shape or form.

meteor The luminous streak seen in the sky when a meteoroid burns up in the atmosphere. Sometimes called a falling star or a shooting star.

meteorite The part of a meteoroid that survives a collision with a planet's atmosphere.

meteoroid A solid object that is located in interplanetary space or is passing through Earth's atmosphere.

meteor shower A display of many meteors, caused when Earth passes through a stream of comet debris.

micrometeorite Dust-sized particles that survive passage through Earth's atmosphere.

minerals Natural substances that are the building blocks of rocks.

nebulae Masses of interstellar dust or gas and dust.

nucleus The central mass of a comet, which is made of ice and dust-sized particles of rock.

observatory A building that houses telescopes, where astronomers view and study space.

orbit The path that an object follows as it repeatedly travels around another object.

parallax An apparent change in the direction of an object caused by a change in the viewer's position.

perihelion The point on a comet's orbit when it is closest to the Sun.

periodic Something that happens at regular time intervals.

planetoid Another name for an asteroid.

radiant A point in the sky from which a meteor appears to come.

short period A term for a comet that circles the Sun every 200 years or less.

solar system The Sun plus all the bodies that orbit it.

solar wind Electrically charged particles that flow outward from the Sun.

theory A belief based on certain ideas and facts.

universe All of the celestial objects that exist in space.

vaporize To be converted into vapor or barely visible matter.

FURTHER READING

Asimov, Isaac. *Comets and Meteors.* Milwaukee, WI: Gareth Stevens, 1989.

———. *How Did We Find Out About Comets?* New York: Walker & Co., 1975.

———. *The Asteroids.* Milwaukee, WI: Gareth Stevens, 1988.

———. *Asteroids.* New York: Dell, 1991.

Brewer, Duncan. *Comets, Asteroids, and Meteorites.* Tarrytown, NY: Marshall Cavendish, 1992.

Carlisle, Madelyn. *Let's Investigate Magical, Mysterious Meteorites*. Hauppage, NY: Barron, 1992.

Hawkes, Nigel. *Mysteries of the Universe*. Brookfield, CT: Millbrook Press, 1994.

Hutchison, Robert, and Graham, Andrew. *Meteorites*. New York: Sterling Press, 1994.

Krupp, Edwin C. *The Comet and You*. New York: Macmillan, 1985.

Lauber, Patricia. *Voyagers from Space: Meteors and Meteorites*. New York: HarperCollins Children's Books, 1989.

Moore, Patrick. *The Guinness Book of Astronomy*, 5th ed. London: Guinness Publishing, 1995.

————. *The Starry Sky*. Brookfield, CT: Millbrook Press, 1994.

Odyssey Magazine, Cobblestone Publishing, Peterborough, NH.

Simon, Seymour. *Comets, Meteors and Asteroids*. New York: Morrow Junior Books, 1994.

Sky & Telescope Magazine, Cambridge, MA.

Sorenson, Lynda. *Comets and Meteors*. Vero Beach, FL: Rourke, 1993.

Walker, Jane. *The Solar System*. Brookfield, CT: Millbrook Press, 1993.

ON-LINE

To get the latest news on comets, visit Charles Boley's Comets On-Line at http://fly.hiwaay.net/~cwbol/astron/comet.html

Visit the NASA home page at http://www.nasa.gov/NASA_homepage.html

The Comet Observation Homepage provides comet information and visual images. Visit it at http://encke.jpl.nasa.gov/

To explore Near-Earth Objects (comets, meteors, and asteroids) go to The NEO Page at http://cfa-www.harvard.edu/cfa/ps/NEO/TheNEOPage.html

SOURCES

Asimov, Isaac. *Comets and Meteors*. Milwaukee, WI: Gareth Stevens, 1990.

———. *How Did We Find Out About Comets?* New York: Walker & Co., 1975.

Barnes-Svarney, Patricia. *Omni*. "Halley's Hiccup." August 1992.

Calder, Nigel. *The Comet Is Coming!* New York: Viking Press, 1980.

Henbest, Nigel. *Comets, Stars, and Planets*. New York: Exeter Books, 1985.

Hoverstein, Paul. "Telescopic Spectacle Streaks Toward Earth." *USA Today*, March 15, 1996.

———. "Comet-Gazers Have a Tail to Tell." *USA Today*, March 25, 1996.

Kaufmann, III, William. *Stars & Nebulas*. San Francisco, CA: W. H. Freeman & Co., 1978.

Knight, David C. *Meteors and Meteorites*. New York: Franklin Watts, 1969.

Krupp, E. C. *The Comet and You*. New York: Macmillan, 1985.

Littmann, Mark, and Yeomans, Donald. *Comet Halley: Once in a Lifetime*. Washington, D.C.: American Chemical Society, 1985.

"The Night Visitor." *Newsweek*, April 1996.

Ronan, Colin A. *The Universe Explained, The Earth-Dweller's Guide to the Mysteries of Space*. New York: Henry Holt, 1994.

Sagan, Carl, and Druyan, Ann. *Comet*. New York: Random House, 1985.

"Three Special Stones." *Sky & Telescope*, February 1996.

"The Unseen Solar System: Hubble Finds the Place 200 Million Comets Call Home." *Discover the World of Science*, November 1995.

Wilford, John Noble. "First Close-Up Photo of Asteroid Released." *New York Times*, November 16, 1991.

Yeomans, Donald. *Comets: A Chronological History of Observation, Science, Myth and Folklore*. New York: John S. Wiley & Sons, 1991.

INDEX